design PAPER

ANTHEA KROOK
JENNY MANSFIELD

63 DESIGNS TO MAKE SCRAPBOOKING EASY

Published by Bay Books an imprint of Murdoch Books Pty Limited. Pier 8/9, 23 Hickson Road, Millers Point NSW 2000, Australia
ISBN 0-681-28953-8. Printed by Sing Cheong Printing Company. Printed in China. First printed 2005.

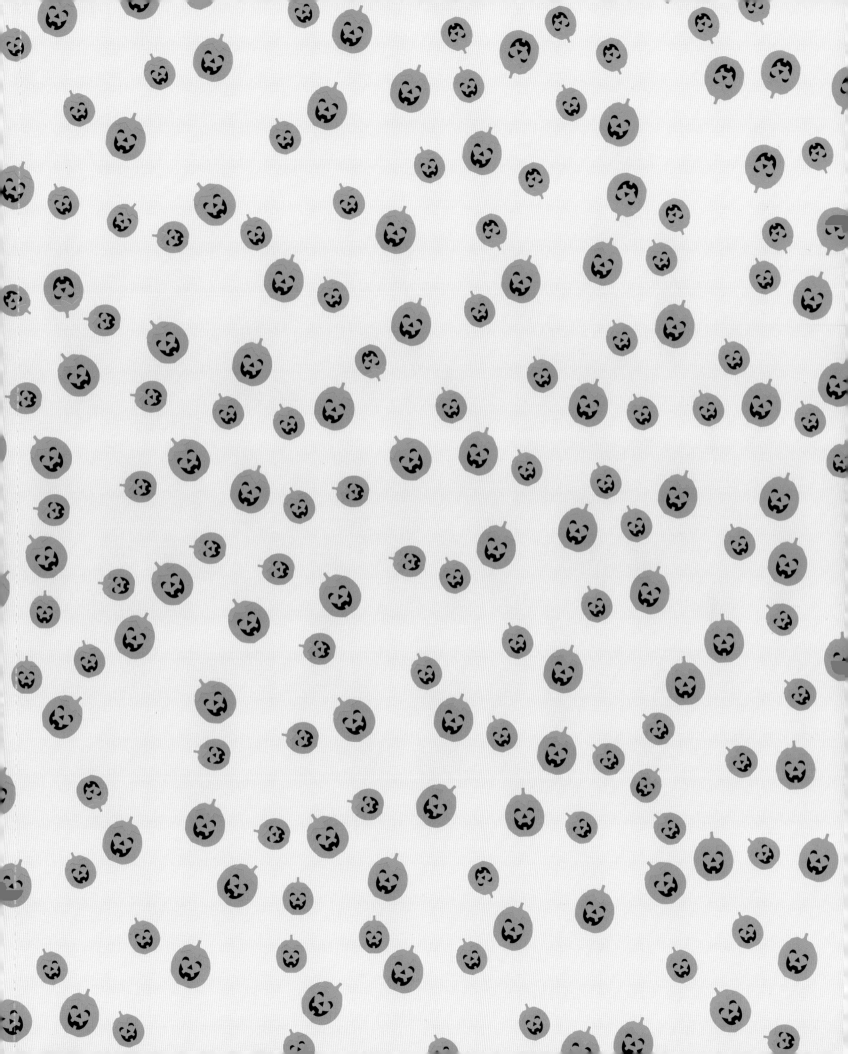

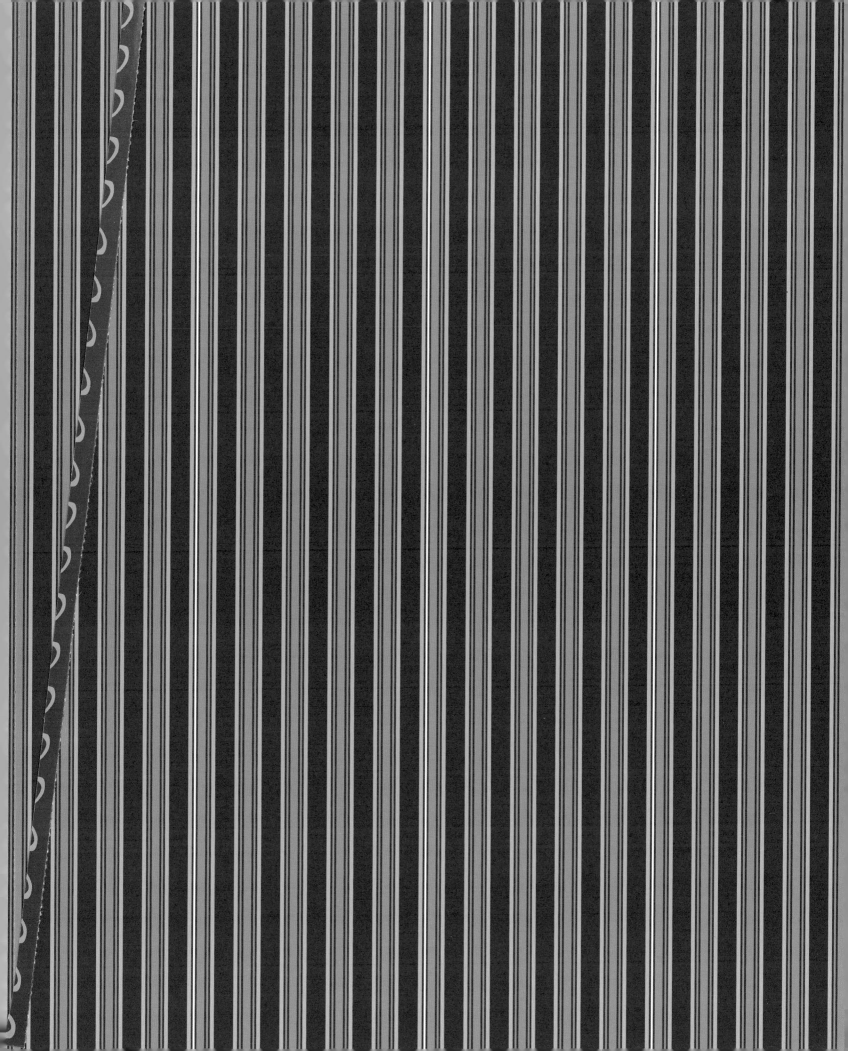

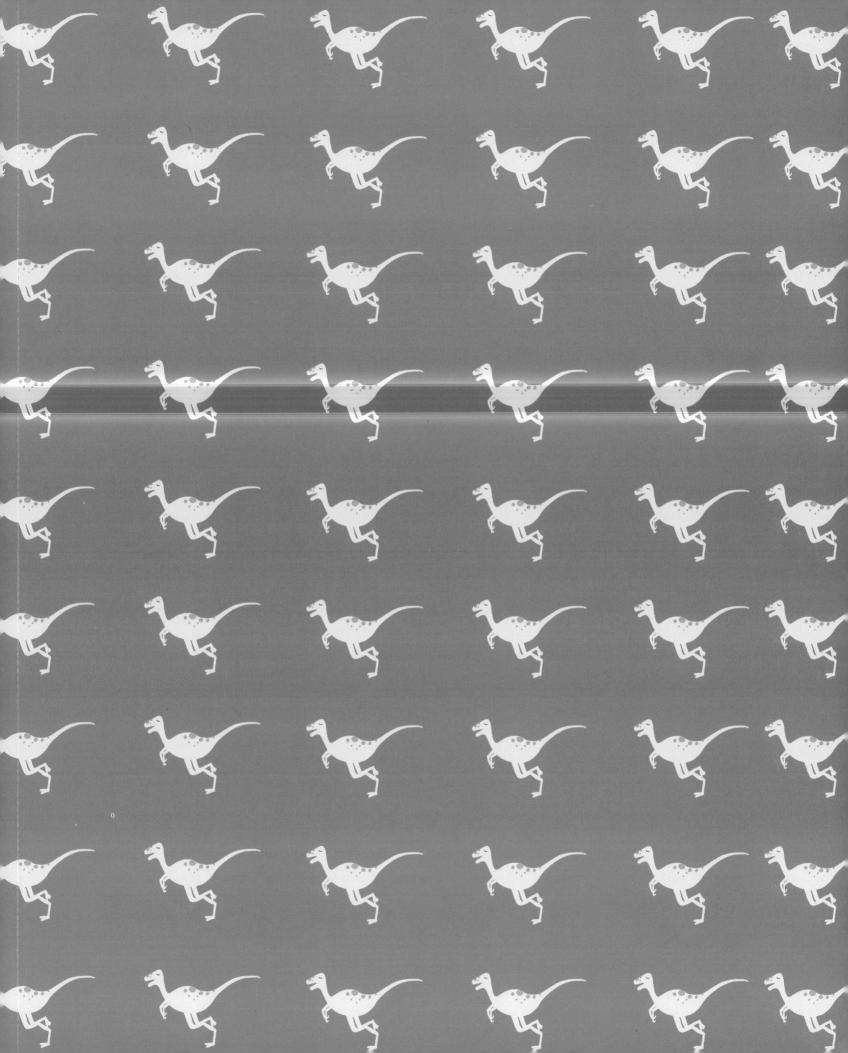

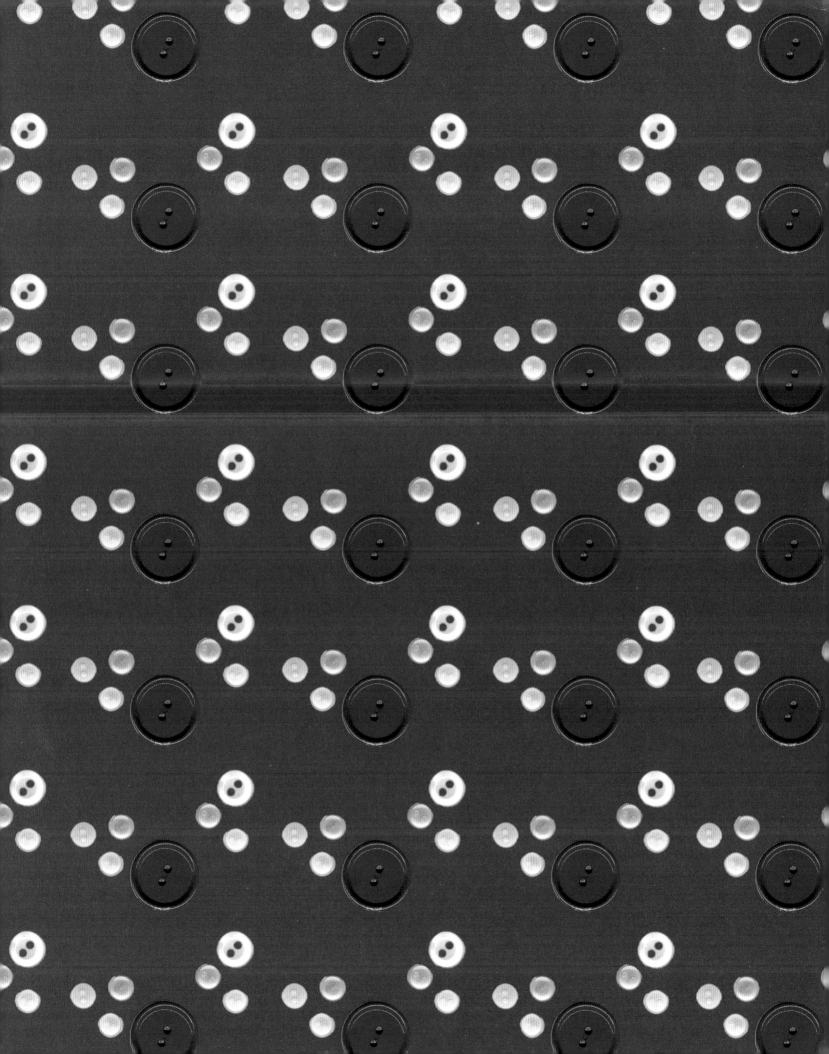

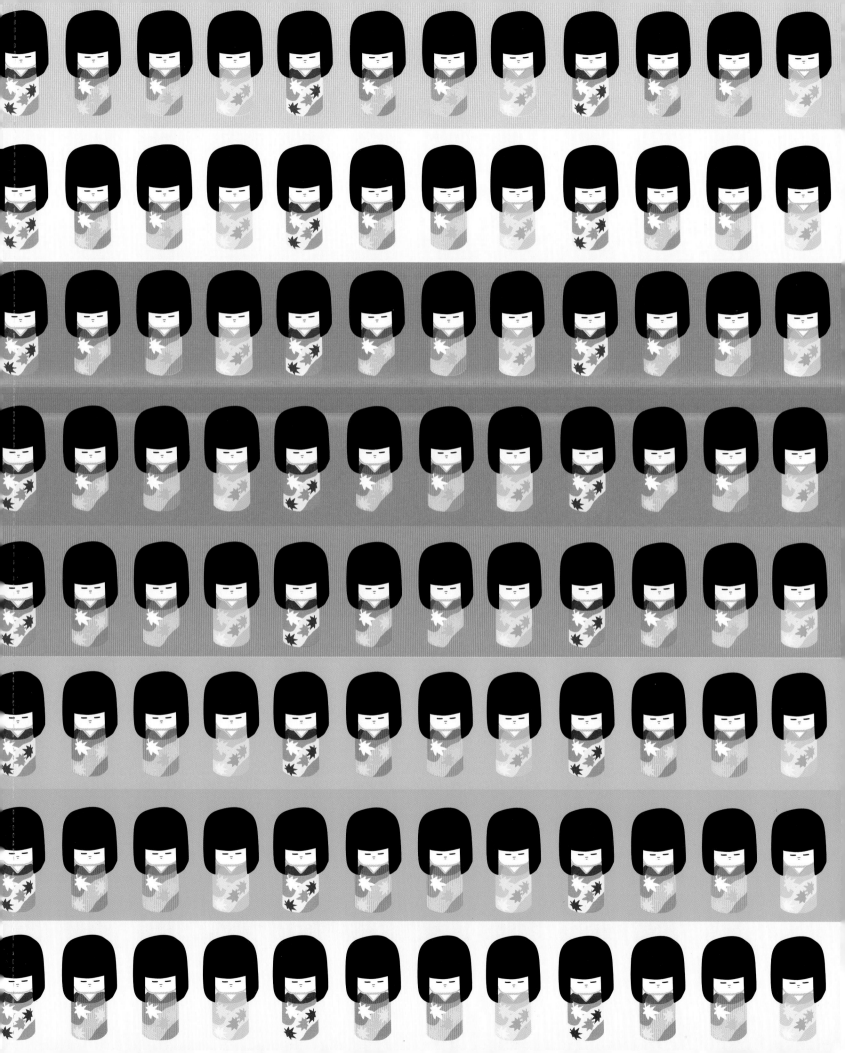

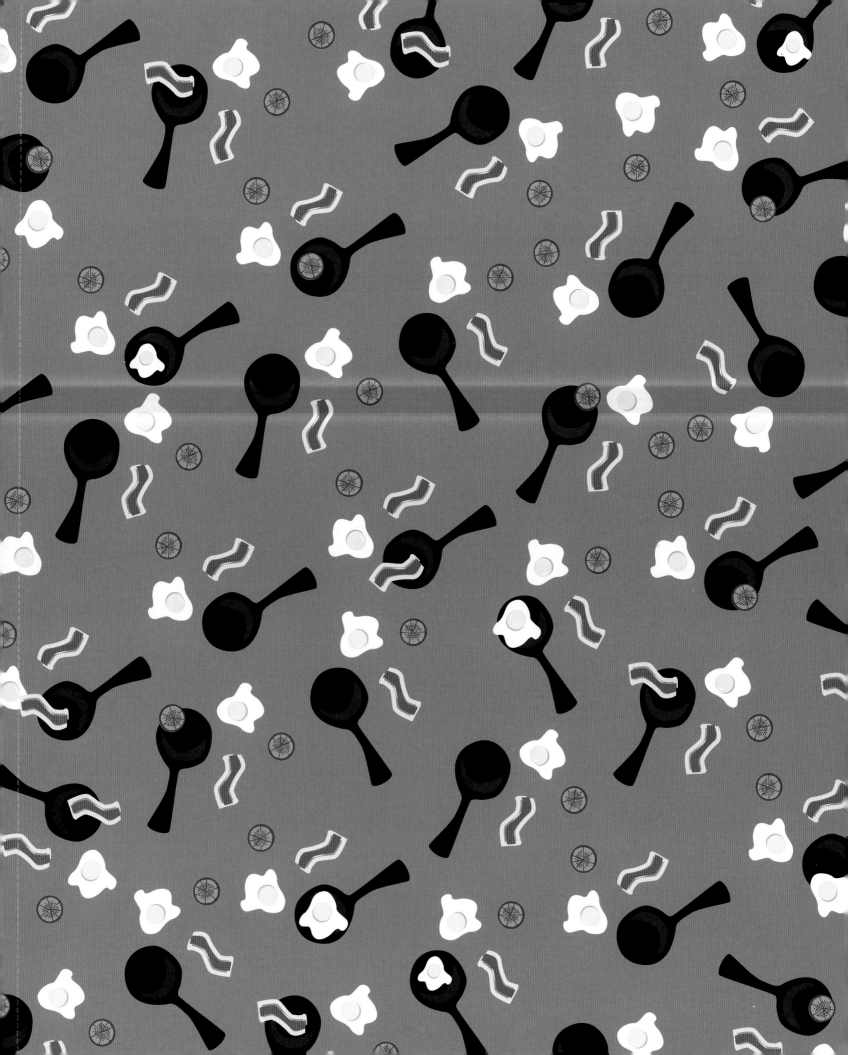

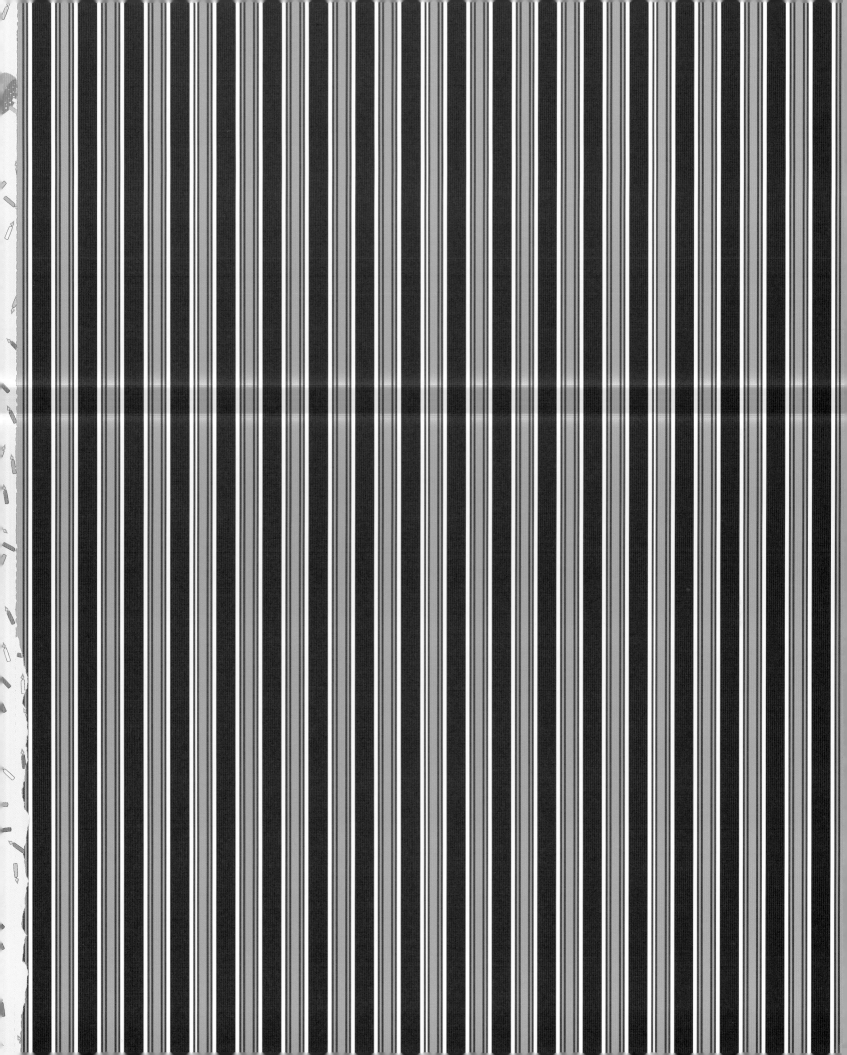

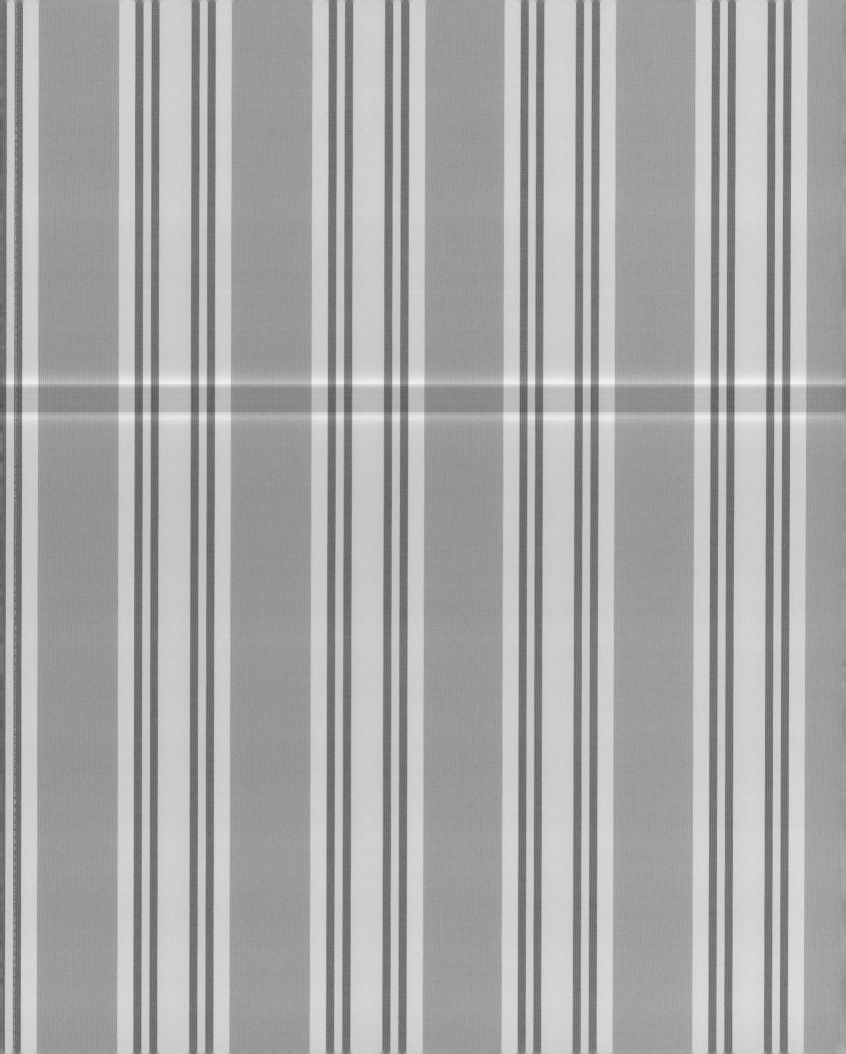

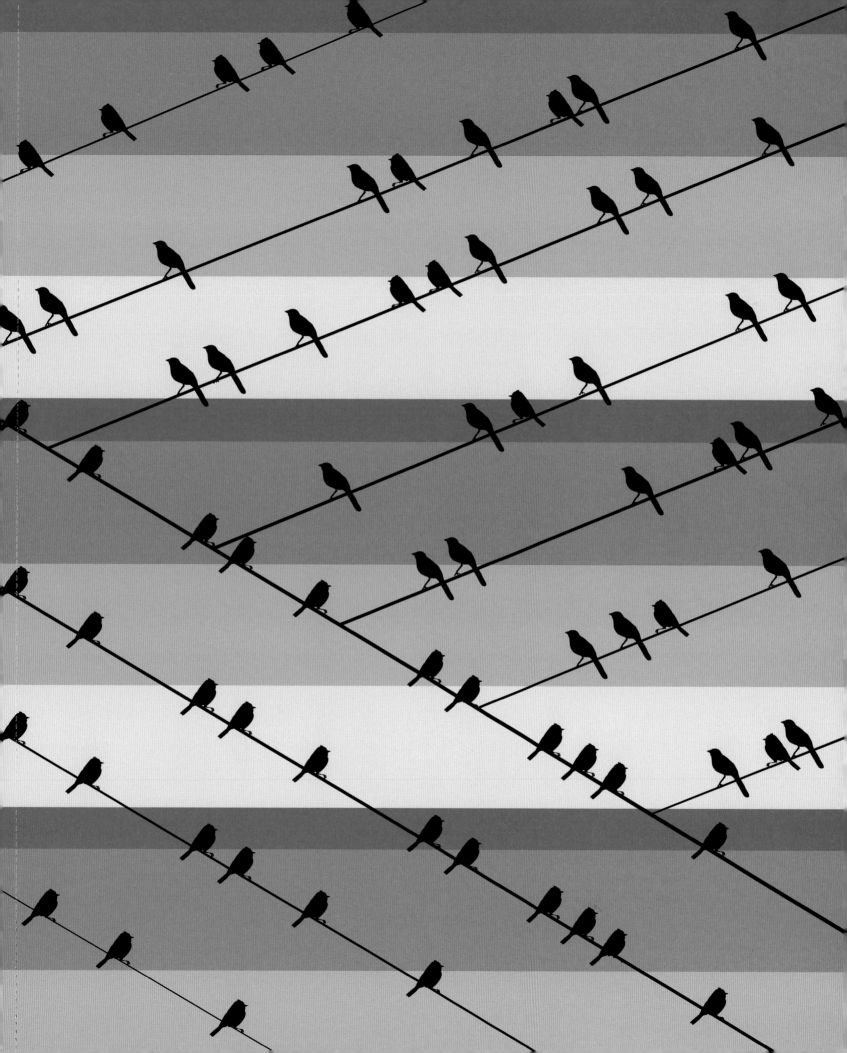

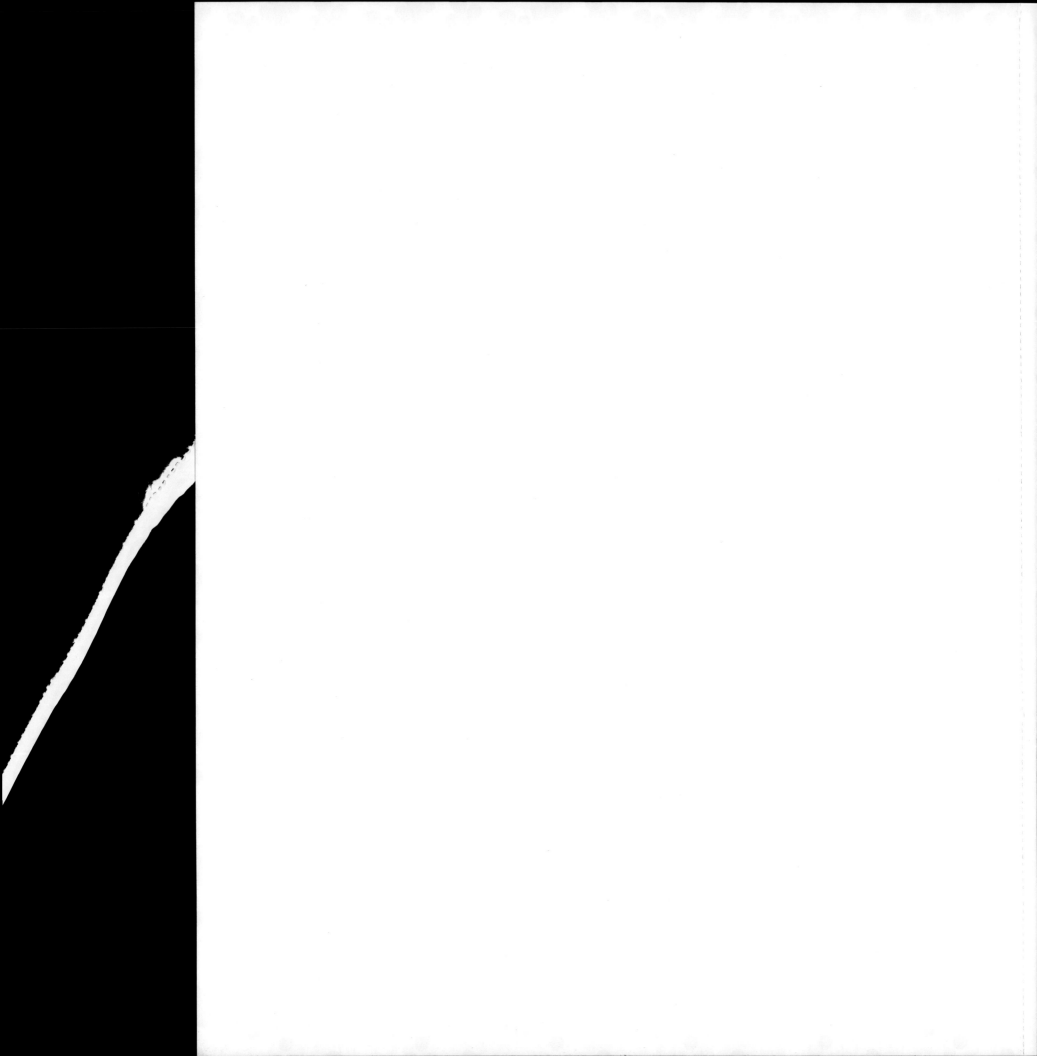

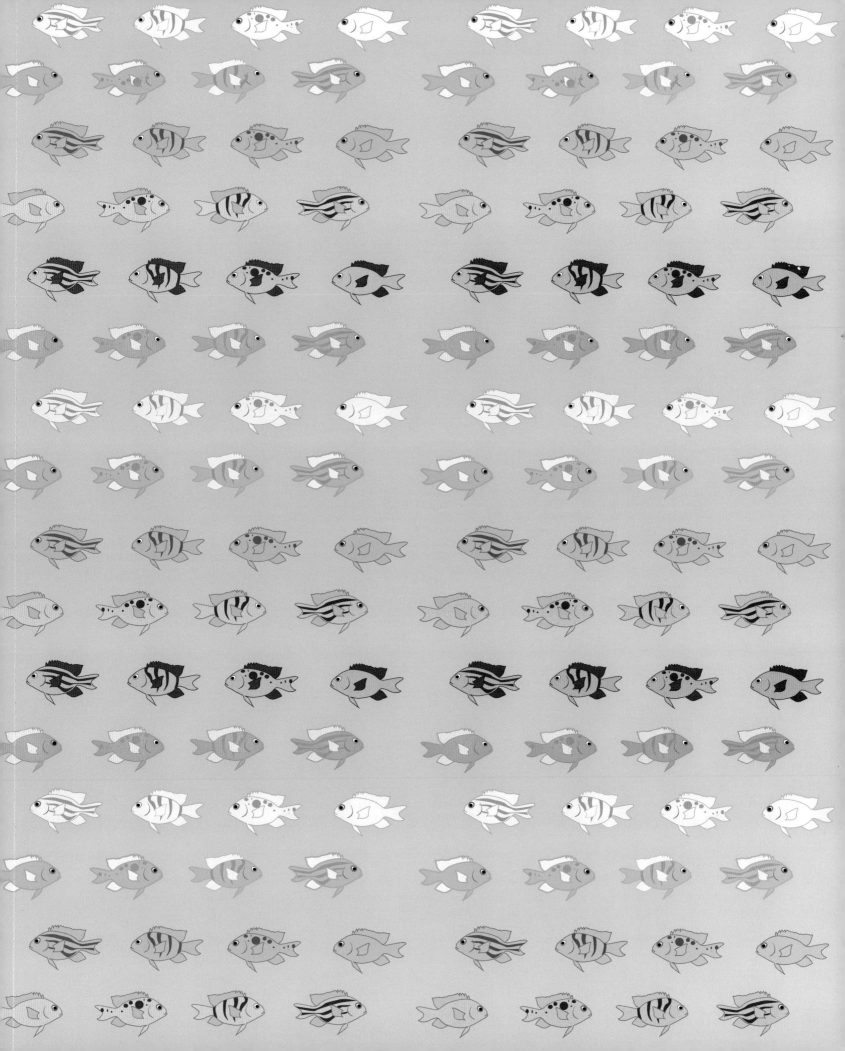

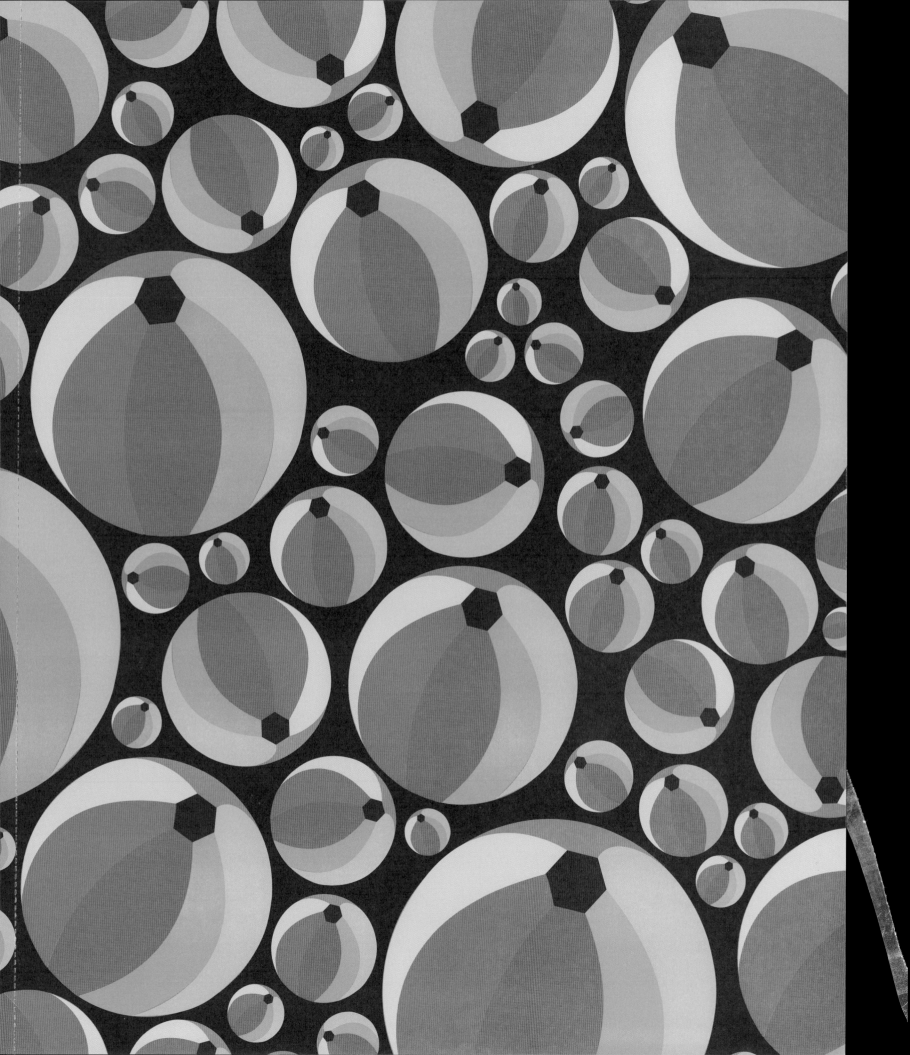

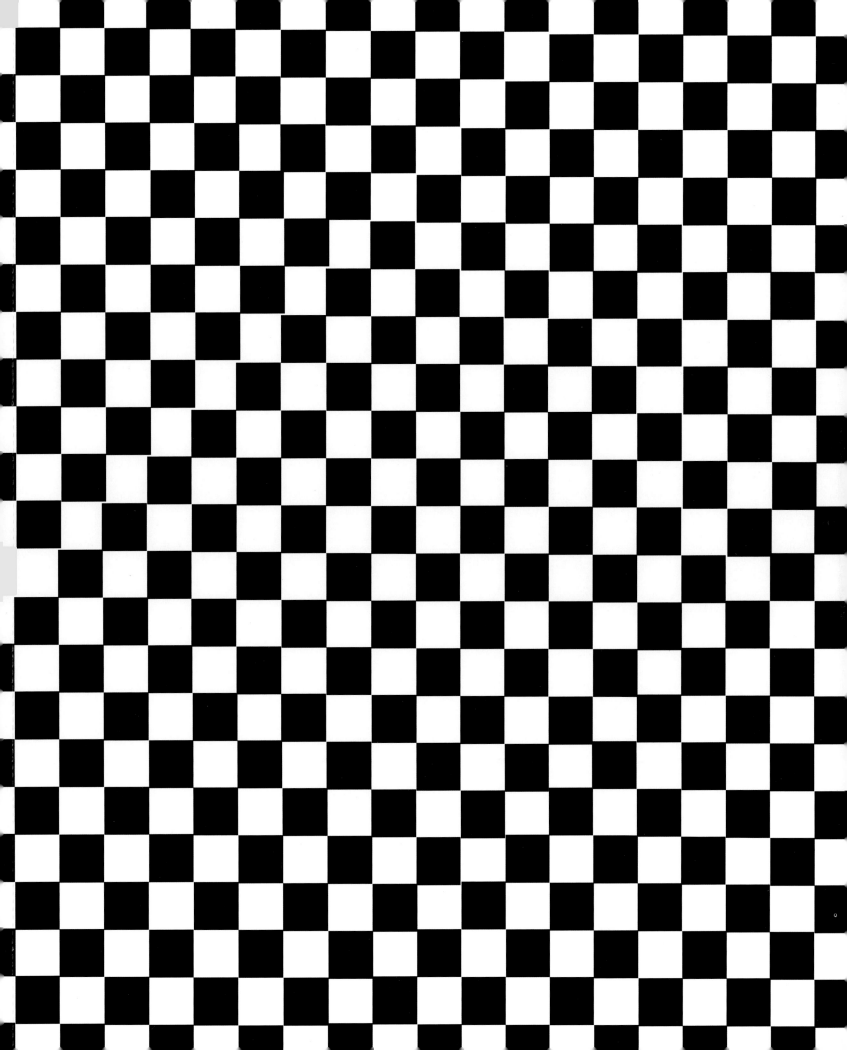

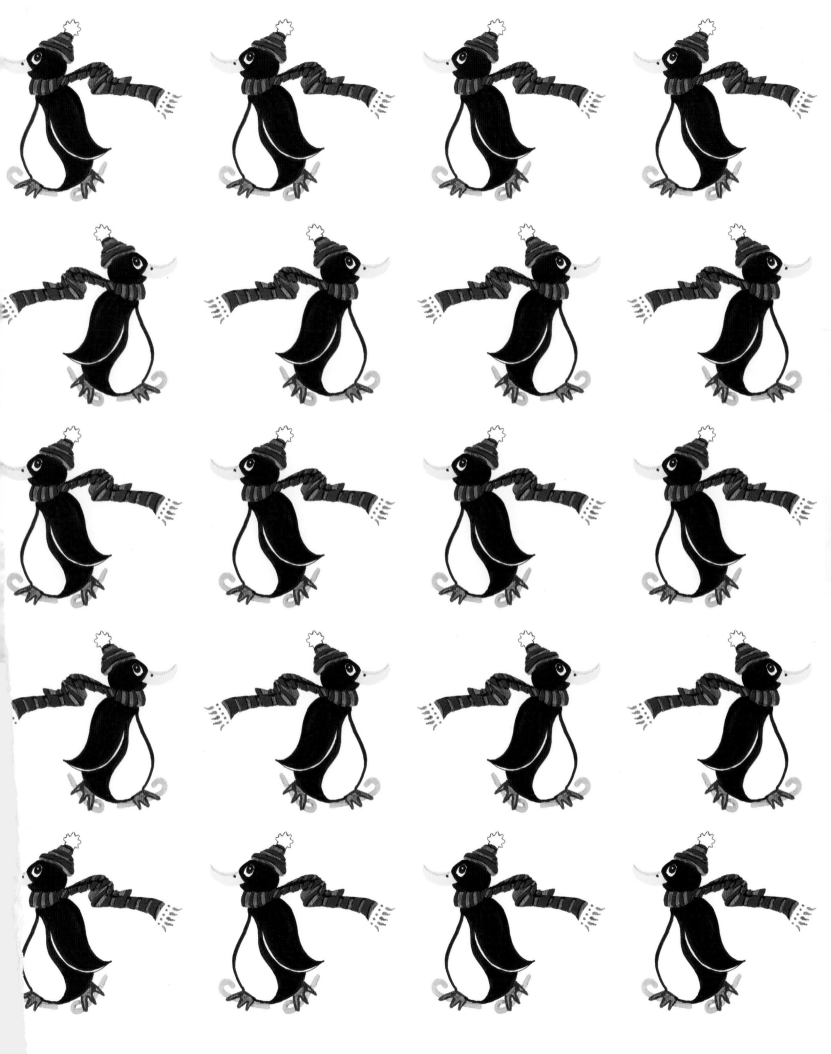